Presented to: Mike and Pam
From: Charles and Jo Rabon
On the Occasion of: the death of your Mother.
Blessings!

The Beauty of Friendship

LLOYD JOHN OGILVIE

The Beauty of Friendship

A Harvest House Special Edition

HARVEST HOUSE PUBLISHERS
Eugene, Oregon 97402

The Beauty of Friendship

Copyright © 1980 by Harvest House Publishers
Eugene, Oregon 97402

Library of Congress Catalog Card Number 80-80463
ISBN 0-89081-243-8

All rights reserved. No portion of this book may be reproduced in any form without the written permission of thge Publisher.

Printed in the United States of America.

Design by Koechel/Peterson Design
Minneapolis, Minnesota 55406

Friendship With God

The beauty of friendship begins with God. The awesome message of the Bible is that the CREATOR, SUSTAINER AND REDEEMER of the universe wants to be our friend.

This is not sloppy subjectivism, it's based on fact. Abraham was called a friend of God (James 2:23). Exodus 33:11 records that Moses spoke with God "as a man speaks to his friend" and Jesus called His disciples friends. Christianity is the cumulative expression of friendship with the Lord.

But just as we cannot comprehend the fatherhood of God by the example of the best of human fathers, so too our friendship with God is so much more than the finest of human friendships. Rather, we learn what it means to be a friend from the kind of friend He is to us. His love is unfailing, His forgiveness offered even before we ask, His presence is with us when we least deserve it. His loyalty is unflinching, His faithfulness is without measure. The only way to learn how to be a friend is to discover friendship with God. His consistency, constancy and compassion will inadvertently transform our attitudes and actions. Want to be a great friend? Become a friend of God!

"No longer do I call you servants, for a servant does not know what his master is doing; but I have called you friends."

John 15:15, NKJB

I'm Glad I'm Me!

I asked a woman for her definition of a friend. She said, "One who helps me say 'I'm glad I'm me!' "A man said, "A friend is a person with whom I feel good about the person who lives inside my skin."

Those definitions prompted an inventory. I asked people how many friends make them feel good about themselves. Many shared the fact that most of their friends are too bound up in their own problems to have much energy left to encourage them. The startling realization made many of those to whom I talked decide to give others what they needed themselves. I should not be amazed that friendships and marriages have been transformed.

John R. Mott said, "The awareness of a need and the capacity to meet that need: this constitutes a call." A Christian has a heavenly calling to help people say, "By God's gift and grace, I'm glad I'm me!"

Victor Hugo said, "The supreme happiness of life is the conviction that we are loved." I would add—loved by God. His love enables a creative self-acceptance and appreciation. True humility is acceptance of God's gifts and giving the glory to Him. A friend is an agent of communicating that sublime conviction. Christ believes in us, knowing all about us. Can we do less?

"Comfort one another and build one another up...."

I Thessalonians 5:11

Friendship for Friendship's Sake

A friend had done me a great favor. I called him to express my gratitude. "Isn't that what friends are for?" he asked. We talked about how drab and difficult life would be without friends to step in to help with impossible situations, open doors for us and use their influence for our advantage.

The danger is that we begin to think of friends for what they have done or can do for us. If the only time we call on them is when we need something, the friendship disintegrates into a quid pro quo of bartered assistance. "I'll help you *if* you help me" is the unspoken message. I overheard an executive's comment when he was told that a "friend" had called. "Wonder what he wants now?" was his guarded response.

Do we care about our friends, not for what we can get but for what we give? What if there were absolutely nothing a friend could accomplish for us? Would we still cherish the relationship? "Friendship for friendship's sake" has become a good corrective for me. It spurs me on to spend time and energy to encourage friends when there is nothing I need. Then opportunities of mutual need are a delight and not a drag.

"We make a living by what we get, but we make a life by what we give."

Winston S. Churchill

"If you love only those who love you, what good is that? Even scoundrels do that much."

Matthew 5:46 TLB

A Special Friend

"The deepest principle in human nature is the craving to be appreciated."
William James

A friend is someone who makes us feel special. We all need the self-esteem that comes when a person helps us to know that we are unique, never-to-be-repeated miracles of God.

What can we do and say to our friends that communicates this dynamic inner assurance? The key is in the word affirmation. Most of us know all about our inadequacies and failures. What we need is friends who believe in us and help us imagine and realize our full potential. It is easy to get down on ourselves and devaluate the special person we were created to be. A friend is a lift, not a load; a boost, not a burden.

The liberating power of affirmation flows from a person who feels of value himself. When we experience the Lord's delight in us and the lengths He was willing to go to show us how special we are, we become people with whom others feel the excitement of their specialness. People who have the gift of self-esteem are able to make their friends feel good about themselves.

If we're not excited about being ourselves, we can be sure no one around us will be excited about himself. The scales of our lives are heavily weighted with self-negation of years of conditioning. We are to be friends who tip the scales with the precious gift of affirmation.

"See how very much our heavenly Father loves us, for He allows us to be called His children—think of it—and we really are."
I John 3:1, TLB

A Six-Way Test of Friendship

Over the years, my understanding of what it means to be a friend and have friends has deepened profoundly. The more I experience friendship with Christ, the more I realize that there are six words, all beginning with an "L", that spell friendship. They provide a helpful, six-way test of the kind of friend we are or can be.

LOVE—A friend loves unconditionally. Friendship is not dependent upon performance or perfection. We are a friend not for what we can get but what we can give.

LOYALTY—True friends can count on each other to be for them, defend each other when others criticize or misunderstand, and remain steadfast in difficulties and discouragements.

LISTENING—We all long to have someone hear what we are saying and what we mean beneath the levels of words.

LAUGHTER—We all get grim when we take ourselves too seriously and fail to take God seriously enough. Without ever laughing at us, a friend helps us to laugh at ourselves.

LONGSUFFERING—Any real friendship endures the test of our failures and foibles. Patience takes the long view and claims what we will be, not what we've been.

"If you love someone you will be loyal to him no matter what the cost. You will always believe in him, always expect the best of him, and always stand your ground in defending him." I Corinthians 13:7, TLB

The Inside Outsider

"If you want to be respected by others, the great thing is to respect yourself."

I overheard a disturbing comment about a lovely woman. "She has a large circle of friends. Too bad it doesn't include herself." What was meant was that the woman had never accepted herself as her own friend. Though she was "Mrs. Put-Together," she put herself down constantly.

Have you ever thought of yourself as a friend? Have you made friends with that inner you? The stranger to most of us is the inside outsider. Ourselves.

When we allow Christ to be our Friend, one of the first things He does is introduce us to our real selves. He wants us to know, accept, love and forgive ourselves. He told us we cannot love our neighbors until we love ourselves. That's not easy. We know all we've been and done.
So does He!

When we yield ourselves to Him, He accepts us as we are but does not leave us there. He begins a never-ending process of making us like Himself. The denial of self He calls for is the denial of our right to control our lives and stay as we are. The self is to be the container and transmitter of the living Christ. We are people in process, and the Lord wants us to enjoy the process. If you wait until you are perfect to accept a friendship with yourself, you may miss one of the greatest friends you could have!

"For all the law is fulfilled in one word, even this: 'You shall love your neighbor as yourself.'"

Galatians 5:14, NKJB

Who Can Share the Joy?

"To God be the glory, great things He hath done."

Fanny Crosby

Who is the first person you think of calling or going to see when you've had a great success or victory? A good determinant of a great friend is that you can share your joys as easily as your sorrows. Everyone needs a cheering section. Genuine friends can enter into our celebration with as much or more enthusiasm as they would have if the fortuitous serendipity had happened to them. A true friend is a maximizer rejoicing and giving God the glory for the great things He has done in our lives.

It takes a lot of confidence to trust our friends with our accomplishments. We assume they are for us and will not confuse our praise with pride. They know that all we have and are is God's gift and they can join us in thanksgiving. There is no envy or competition. They are so secure in their own gifts that they can celebrate us.

Questions linger and demand answers. Am I that kind of friend? Do people know I am pulling for them? What keeps me from being enthusiastic when others succeed? Can I give God glory and not worry about getting the glory?

"Do everything for the glory of God."
I Corinthians 10:31, TLB

Better Than Our Best

"It is more effective to spend time talking to Christ about a man than talking to a man about Christ, because if you are talking to Christ about a man earnestly, trustingly, in the course of time you cannot help talking to the man effectively about Christ."

Robert Boyd Munger

Friendship is sharing life in all its difficulties and delights. A friend is one to whom you can open your heart completely and unburden what's happening to and around you. He or she will try to understand and then draw from experience to give insight or advice.

But our human resources are limited. Our counsel is so often confused by our own perspective and preconceptions. More than advice, we all need God. An honest friend is able to admit his limitations, pray with us and then pray at length for us. Wisdom is so much better than sagacity. Wisdom comes only as we pray.

The other day, a friend shared a problem. None of the alternatives was attractive. The dangers were alarming. My temptation was to tell him what I thought. Then I overcame my desire to be his "answer man." I told him that I wanted to spend as much time talking to God about the problem as we had spent talking about it. The result was guidance from the Lord that revealed a direction I could never have envisioned. My friend was blessed. And so was I!

"Share each other's troubles and problems, and so obey the Lord's command."
Galatians 6:2, TLB

Caring Is Everything

When the great mystic, philosopher and saint, Von Hugel, lay dying, his niece noticed that his lips were moving. She could not hear what he was trying to say, so she put her ear close to his mouth. What she heard was this:

"Caring is everything; nothing matters but caring." Caring is friendship in action. A caring friend is a precious gift.

At the close of a retreat some time ago we sang the refrain, "He careth for you. He careth for you. Through sunshine or shadow, He careth for you." Then we turned to the people around us and sang it again, changing the pronoun from "He" to "I." Tears streamed down many faces as people sang what they felt so deeply: "I care for you."

But the real test of that moving expression of friendship was in what happened in the weeks and months that followed. We made prayer lists of one another's names. Caring was expressed in daily prayer. The people kept in touch with one another and were available to one another in time of need. Time, involvement and resources were shared unselfishly.

Barriers were broken down as people opened their hearts and homes. The motto of the group became:
"God cares, and so do I!"

"Be kindly affectionate to one another with brotherly love, in honor giving preference to one another, not lagging in diligence, fervent in spirit serving the Lord; rejoicing in hope, patient in tribulation, continuing steadfastly in prayer; distributing to the needs of the saints, given to hospitality."

Romans 12:10-13, NKJB

"I'm Praying for You!"

"There is nothing that makes us love a man so much as praying for him."

William Law

The most profound expression of friendship is prayer. There are no more encouraging words we can say or hear than, "I am praying for you!" God has entrusted us with the mighty power of intercessory prayer. It is a gift. We become partners with Him in the accomplishment of His purposes in the lives of our friends.

Prayer enables us to share the pulsebeat of the heart of God. The more we pray for our friends, the more we will be able to love them as He does. To intercede means to pass between, to go to God on behalf of a friend and then to go to him or her with the blessing of the wisdom and guidance of God.

But intercessory prayer is more than convincing God of what we think our friends need. Prayer is listening with two ears: one to our friends to discern the real need beneath the surface of a problem or potential; the other to God to receive His guidance for what we are to pray. Prayer begins with God. He calls us into fellowship with Him so that He can inspire us to pray for what He is more ready to give than we are daring enough to ask. Intercessory prayer is not overcoming God's reluctance but accepting His unlimited resources.

"Likewise the Spirit also helps us...for we do not know what we should pray for as we ought, but the Spirit Himself makes intercession for us...."

Romans 8:26, NKJB

Jesus said, "Ask and you will receive, that your joy may be full."

John 16:24, NKJB

I Cannot Let You Go!

**"O Love that wilt not let me go,
I rest my weary soul in Thee.
I give Thee back the life I owe,
That in its ocean depths its flow
May richer, fuller be."**

George Matheson

When George Matheson was going blind, his fiancée told him that she would not marry him. His world collapsed temporarily. Then, as his faith in God was deepened by this disappointment, he picked up his pen and wrote the verse we just read. It is now part of a lovely hymn which gives courage and hope to those who need to know that, when life tumbles in, God will not let us go.

A friend is one who can say, "God will not let me go, and there is nothing that will ever allow me to let you go." When we have friends like that, we may be knocked down, but never knocked out. What a poet said of his beloved, God says to us and we can say to one another.

"Love...bears all things, believes all things, hopes all things, endures all things. Love never fails...."

I Corinthians 13:7-8, ASV

The Blight of Gossip

"To speak ill of others is a dishonest way of praising ourselves."

Will Durant

Nothing blights the beauty of a friendship more quickly than gossip. When a friend gossips to you about another person, there is always the lingering suspicion that he or she will do the same about you. Friendship is based on mutual acceptance. We entrust ourselves to friends whom we know will keep our confidences. A budding friendship is often withered when a person draws us into destructive analysis of someone else. We begin to feel uneasy, guarded, defensive. Our concern is to say or do nothing which could be used against us. The friendship soon is strained and reserved. The Spanish proverb is right: "Whoever gossips to you will gossip of you."

A sure cure for gossip is to never say anything about another we have not said to that person or are willing to say within twenty-four hours. Often we need a friend to talk out our feelings about another person. But that can never be a substitute for honest and loving confrontation with the person. A helpful friend is one who can listen, enable us to clarify our feelings about another, and then press us to discern what we can do to be creative instead of critical.

"Let us therefore stop turning critical eyes on one another. If we must be critical, let us be critical of our own conduct and see that we do nothing to make a brother stumble or fall."

Romans 14:13, Phillips

The Triple-Braided Cord

"One, plus one, plus one, equals one."

Louis H. Evans, Sr.

"And one standing alone can be attacked and defeated, but two can stand back to back and conquer; three are even better, for a triple-braided cord is not easily broken."

Ecclesiastes 4:12, TLB

Christian friendship is a triple-braided cord. One friend, plus another, plus Christ, makes the cord not easily broken. Bonhoeffer said that there are no direct Christian relationships. We go through Christ to each other. The Christ in a friend is stronger than the Christ in us and strengthens the Christ in us. When Christ is the third strand of the triple-braided cord, we are able to love and forgive each other with His power.

Our commitment to Christ binds us irrevocably to each other. We find our oneness in Him. We begin to think, feel, hope and work with unity of purpose and direction. When Christ is the source and center of a friendship, forces to pull us apart are impotent. There is the buffer of Christ's grace when we fail or disappoint each other. We belong to Him and each other in spite of what happens around us. Pressures may strain the cord but cannot break it. We will experience the fulfillment of Christ's prayer:

"Father, keep through Your name these whom You have given Me, that they may be one as We are."

John 17:11, NKJB

Don't Turn Me Off!

"The continuance of anger is hatred."

Frances Quarles

*T*here was a strange note stuck on the dashboard of a friend's car. "Dear Roger: What do you turn off before you turn off the ignition?" I asked my friend what it meant. He explained that he had a bad habit of turning the ignition off before he had turned off the heater, radio and lights. Later, when he would turn the ignition on again, it would drain the battery. His wife had attached the question as a reminder.

The question lingered in my mind long afterward. It gave me a living parable. We turn people off, little by little, before we get turned off by them. What do you turn off before you turn your friends off? The things people do and say often distress us. We become inwardly impatient. One thing is added to another until we have a pile of resentments. Before we know it, we have cut off any deep communication.

It is impossible not to be distressed by the things our friends do. Great friends keep short accounts. They deal with their feelings day by day rather than building up a resentment reservoir. Just as God's grace for us is fresh every morning, so we need to couple the expression of our feelings with forgiveness. Love and honesty are inseparable in an ever-deepening friendship. Get it out; get it healed; get it over!

"Don't let the sun go down on your anger."
Ephesians 4:26, RSV

Be That Kind of Friend

"The only way to have a friend is to be one."

Emerson

A college student complained that she had few real friends. "What kind of friends would you like?" asked a wise Christian counselor. The young woman listed the qualities she wanted in friends. She wanted them to be faithful, loyal, caring, and share her commitment to Christ. "Then be that kind of friend to others, and you will never lack true friends again," the counselor suggested. The advice was simple, yet the secret of developing enriching friendships.

In a lonely world, it's tragic to be lonely alone. Everyone longs for the same kind of friendships. A Christian is an imitator. Having been loved by Christ, we are set free to reach out to others. Life will never be boring or lonely. We will have more friends than we ever dreamed possible.

Jesus' Golden Rule encourages us to do to others what we want them to do to us. Our difficulty is in picturing what we need others to do for us. We expect little and are not disappointed. When we experience the Lord's unlimited generosity, we begin to appreciate what a loving friend is like. A friendship revolution is started when we dare to be to others what He has been to us.

"Therefore, whatever you want men to do to you, you also do to them, for this is the Law and the Prophets."

Matthew 7:12, NKJB

Plankated Vision

The icy body language between the husband and wife spoke volumes. They had come to see me about the lack of communication in their marriage. They sat at opposite ends of the couch in my study. I asked each of them what was happening to their marriage. The husband went first. "Criticize, criticize, criticize!" he blurted out. "All she does is criticize!" I looked over at the wife, inviting her analysis. "Judge, judge, judge!" she said angrily, "All *he* ever does is judge!" Then she went on to say, "My criticisms are not half as bad as his judgments!"

Which would you say is the worst? Cankerous criticism or jaundiced judgment? Actually, neither was in any position to judge or criticize. They were both insecure, loveless people who were stabilizing the frustration inside them by lambasting each other. Nothing can destroy a marriage or a friendship more quickly than judgmentalism or constant criticism.

Most of us have plankated vision. We have a plank in our own eye and judge the speck in another's eye. Jesus tells us to take the plank out of our own eye and then we will be able to help a friend with the speck in his eye. Once we allow the Lord to help us with our planks, we will be enabled to tenderly and graciously help people with their problems rather than being censorious sources of problems.

"Judge not, that you be not judged. For with the judgment you judge, you will be judged; and with the same measure you use, it will be measured back to you."
Matthew 7:1-2, NKJB

"Beforehand Love"

**"I've found a Friend, Oh such a Friend.
He loved me ere I knew Him;
He drew me with the cords of love,
And thus He bound me to Him.
And round my heart still closely twine
Those ties which naught can sever,
For I am His, and He is mine
Forever and forever.**"

James G. Small

One of the most powerful words which explain Christ's friendship is prevenance. It means "beforehand love." The hymn expresses it beautifully. The Lord chooses us and calls us to be His friends. We find Him as a friend because He has already befriended us. We can come to Him because He first comes to us. He draws us to Himself, and nothing we can do or say will break the ties of His unchanging love. That's our assurance—now and forever. The experience of His friendship makes us want to discover and do His will. Our whole life is set free of compulsion and now is motivated by the liberating confidence of prevenient grace. What a wonderful way to live!

*"You have not chosen Me,
but I have chosen you...."*

John 15:16, NKJB

In Good Repair

"A man, sir, should keep his friendships in constant repair."

Samuel Johnson

Life is dynamic, not static. The only consistent thing is change. We are constantly changing, facing new problems and opportunities. As we change, so do our relationships. None of us is the person he or she was and, thank God, will be as the future unfolds.

A great friendship is one that gives people the freedom to grow and keeps up with their progress. It is no compliment to say to a friend, "You haven't changed a bit!" We know that's meant to be an affirmation of a person's consistency in personal attributes. But are we also aware of the advancements our friends have made as they have turned life's struggles into stepping stones? A friendship that's kept in repair is one in which we are in touch with what a person is learning on all levels of life.

When we say, "How are you, friend?" we should be ready to share the excitement of discoveries battled for and won. It is so easy to lose contact with friends even when they are not separated by distance or time. The Apostle Paul's letters to his friends were filled with his delight over their growth. He kept his friendships in good repair. Listen to what he wrote to his friends in Philippi:

"I thank my God upon my remembrance of you, always in every prayer...making request for you...being confident...that He who began a good work in you will complete it until the day of Jesus Christ...."
Phillipians 1:3-6, NKJB

A Friend, Indeed!

"Hush, I pray you! what if this friend happens to be—God?"

Robert Browning, *Fears and Scruples*

It is an awesome, challenging thought. The Lord comes to us in our friends. What we do and are to them is an expression of what we are to Him. This was the thrust of an alarming message Jesus gave at the conclusion of His ministry. "Assuredly, I say to you, inasmuch as you have done it to one of the least of these My brethren, you have done it to Me." He defined the least as the hungry, the thirsty, the strangers, the sick and the imprisoned. But in the context of His total message, we understand that Jesus wants us to relate to all people as we might receive Him. Everyone is in need in some way.

This is a good litmus test of friendship. It is an incisive inventory of how to evaluate our actions and reactions to people. What would happen if we treated all people as friends and all as if they were the Lord Himself? Try it today. It will transform relationships into an exciting adventure.

"Come, you blessed of My Father, inherit the kingdom prepared for you from the foundation of the world; for I was hungry and you gave me food; I was thirsty and you gave me drink; I was a stranger and you took Me in...."

Matthew 25:34-35 NKJB

A Friend Who Won't Go Away

My definition of a friend is one who knows all about you and won't go away.

How many friends do you have like that? How many people could count on you to be that kind of friend?

So many people are afraid of others knowing them because they suspect that if the truth were known, the friendship would end or, what's worse, become superficial. We keep our thoughts and feelings hidden in fear of censorious judgment. The tragedy is that most people have the same inner secrets. A friend is a person who can dare to be vulnerable about himself so that we feel free to be honest about ourselves. When we spend our energies putting up fronts of pretense, we close out our friends and keep them from being authentic with us.

Something...Someone must break the syndrome. His name is Jesus Christ. He knows all about us and will never go away. The more we know Him in intimate friendship, the more free we become to be open about our needs and inadequacies with others. They begin to feel at ease with us. When we feel sure of Christ we can dare to communicate indefatigable acceptance of others. They will be able to say, "There's one person whom I can trust. His friendship is so profound that there is nothing that would make him go away!"

"For He Himself said, 'I will never leave you nor forsake you.' So that we may boldly say: 'The Lord is my helper, and I will not fear.'"

Hebrews 13:5-6, NKJB

Fellow Adventurers

We are all in the process of becoming what we imagine. Imagination is the power to form, hold and achieve the images of the mind. God has given us imaginations to capture His picture of the persons we were meant to be. Often the best way to "get the picture" is to imagine what we would be like if we were totally surrendered to our Lord, filled with His Spirit, guided by His will, reformed in His image. Imagine it! Think about your relationships, attitudes, countenance, personality.

A friend is a fellow adventurer who can help us throw caution and reserve to the wind and discover what we were like in the mind of God when He first thought of us. In times of indecision, we need friends who can help us get the vision of God's maximum into focus. An adventuresome friend will help us do more than solve problems. He or she will enable us to grasp the potential of God's dream. Most of us plan our lives around our strengths and abilities. What are you attempting that you couldn't do without the energizing power of the Holy Spirit?

"What would you do if you knew you could not fail?"

Bruce Larson

"Let us hold fast the confession of our hope without wavering, for He who promised is faithful. And let us consider how to stimulate one another to love and good deeds." *Hebrews 10:23-24, ASV*

"Do It Now Day"

"I will pass through this world but once. If therefore, there be any kindness I can show or any good thing I can do, let me do it now; let me not defer it or neglect it, for I shall not pass this way again."

Etienne De Grellet

The other day, I called a friend to find out how he was doing. "Just great!" he responded exuberantly. I inquired about the cause of his delight. He told me that he had just finished a "Do it now day." "A what?" I exclaimed. "Well," he explained, "I'm a procrastinator, and after awhile all the unfinished and neglected things I need to do get at me. Then I must set aside a day to clean up what I've put off. I feel great now that I'm back on the track."

Great friendships require "Do it now" days. Action is the final step of learning —and loving. It is easy to put off expressing our affection and concern. Friends begin to wonder if we care, really. No one wants to be taken for granted. A phone call, a letter, or a specific expression of love in action is to a friendship what oxygen is to the lungs, or food to the body.

Mark Twain said, "Never put off until tomorrow what you can do the day after tomorrow." Bad advice! There is a special moment when thought about and feeling for a friend converge and, unless we act, we may never have another chance.

"I have always thought the actions of men the best interpreters of their thoughts."
John Locke

"Whatever your hand finds to do, do it with your might."
Ecclesiastes 9:10, RSV

Friends in Sorrow

"Henceforth there shall be such a oneness that when one weeps the other will taste salt."

Martin Buxbaum

A true friend is a special gift in a time of sorrow. When grief breaks our hearts, we need a friend to share the pain. The old saying is on target: "A sorrow shared is a sorrow halved." An authentic friend will listen and absorb the anguish. Spencer said, "He oft finds present help who does his griefs impart."

There is remedial therapy in talking out our real feelings. But only a friend will give us the freedom to talk until we know what we mean. Often we feel self-pity, anger and indignation in times of grief. The last thing we need is someone to say, "Time heals everything." Time has never healed anything. Love heals everything!

The one thing we can say about our feelings is that they are ours. They may not be very spiritual or rational or magnanimous, but they are an expression of our wounded hearts. A friend will encourage us to get our feelings out and never hold us to them or react to us on the basis of them in the future.

"Give sorrow words; the grief that does not speak, whispers the o'er-fraught heart and bids it break."
                Macbeth, Act IV, Scene 3

"When others are happy, be happy with them. If they are sad, share their sorrow."
                Romans 12:15, TLB

A Place for Broken Hearts

**"And God who gives beginnings
gives the end;
A place for broken things
too broken to mend."**

John Masefield

A woman whose friend had broken her heart said, "If I never see her again, it will be too soon!" Friends can break our hearts. Our capacity to love makes us vulnerable to be hurt. What trusted friends do or say wounds us deeply. Like this woman, we try to write them off, but we can't get them off our memories. Each time we are reminded, all the turbulent feelings tumble about inside us. The wounds are torn open. What can we do with our broken relationships?

The heart of God is the place for broken things too "broke" to mend. And at the center of His heart is the cross. We are reminded of all the times we have broken His heart. He helps us see that people do what they do because of what they are and that what they are cannot be changed without forgiving love. He asks us to relinquish the hurt to Him unreservedly. Then He gives us the power to forgive as He has forgiven us. After that we can go to the person who has hurt us and be the initial reconciler. For God, there is nothing too "broke" to mend!

"The Lord is near to the brokenhearted, and saves the crushed in spirit."
       Psalm 34:18, RSV

"He heals the brokenhearted, and binds up their wounds."
       Psalm 147:3, RSV

Beyond Sympathy

There's a great difference between sympathy and empathy. Sympathy is concern at a distance. Empathy is strong identification. Halford Luccock has defined it as "your pain in my heart."

We all need empathetical friends who will listen long enough to feel our frustrations and fears, hurts and hopes. We want more than an aloof, "I'm sorry, tough luck!"

Empathy is really mercy. The Hebrew word for mercy means to get inside another person's skin to feel what he or she is feeling, hoping, enduring. It requires that we set aside our qualifications, judgments and expectations for another person so that we can mercifully share the burden or challenge.

We must ask ourselves: What can I say, do and be to communicate that I understand? It is only after we have earned the right through empathy that we can offer our insight and wisdom. Moreover, our advice must be tempered in the fires of our own similar experiences. How many of your friends have felt empathy from you? Who needs to know today that their pain is in your heart?

"Mercy is as beautiful in a time of trouble
as rain clouds in a time of drought."
Ecclesiasticus 35:20, Goodspeed

There will be no mercy to those
who have shown no mercy."
James 2:13, TLB

"Blessed are the merciful,
for they shall obtain mercy."

A Good Forgettery

"Remember to forget."

Immanuel Kant

I have a friend who has what he calls a highly trained "forgettery." The word is not in the dictionaries, but it should be. My friend makes a conscious effort to forget the slights and oversights done to him. He feels it's a qualification of friendship. I've tested him several times to see if he can recall the hurt of some harm done to him. All he will say is, "I don't remember anything about that except when I decided to forget it."

Henri Bergson, the French philosopher, once said, "It is the function of the brain to enable us not to remember, but to forget." We laugh at that and say, "I must have a spectacular brain. I'm very forgetful." But there's a real difference between being forgetful and being able to forget painful memories. A good forgettery is developed by a gracious capacity to forgive.

God is the only reliable guide to healthy forgetting and creative remembering. He tells us that when we seek His forgiveness, He will not remember our sins and failures. When we know He has forgotten, we can forget. Then we will be tender in forgetting what others have said or done to us. We will be able to say with Joseph, "God has made me forget..." (Genesis 41:51, ASV). God will help us erase from our minds what will destroy a friendship and will bring to our remembrance the motivating power of His love.

"I will never again remember their sins."
Hebrews 10:17, TLB

The Tie That Unbinds

"We find freedom when we find God; we lose it when we lose Him."

Paul E. Scherer

A man offered, "What can I do for you?" His friend responded playfully, "What did you have in mind?" We smile at that. So often a friend's offer to help us is a desire to control. We all long to have friends who respect us and give us freedom to be ourselves.

A real friend has no strings, no binding preconceptions, not limiting agendas. But that kind of freedom must be rooted in a lively confidence in God. When we trust Him in our friends we can relax, be available to share what He is revealing to them. The old song is wrong. It should be "Blest be the Tie That Unbinds." The bond of love releases people.

We can be free with our friends only after we have become free people. When Christ sets us free from anxiety, fear and worry we become winsome friends who model what life was meant to be. Our task is to live what we wish our friends would experience. We can't give away what we don't have. Nothing can happen through us which has not happened to us. Freedom in Christ is contagious. It's not taught; it's caught.

"Where the Spirit of the Lord is
there is freedom."

II Corinthians 3:17, RSV

Theotelepathy

"One human spirit can, by its power and love, touch another human spirit. It can take the soul and lift it into the atmosphere of God...Those in need of help will find that the praying person is a transmitter of the redeeming power of God. There is actually a mysterious interpenetration of all living souls."

Evelyn Underhill

I want to establish a new word for the beauty of friendship—theotelepathy. It's a combination of telepathy and theopathy.

Telepathy is the communication of one mind with another at a distance by other than sensory means; *i.e.*, contact beyond the physical senses of sight, touch and hearing of proximity. *Tele* means "distance." *Pathy*, from the root of the Greek *paschein*, passion, means "to suffer or feel deeply for, or on behalf of, another." Sympathy and empathy come from this stem.

Theopathy, on the other hand, is spiritual emotion aroused by meditation on God. Prayer. We feel the pathy of God; His love, passion and suffering concern. *Theo* means "God" in Greek. The word theology is a combination of *theo* and *logos*: God and word; thus, a word or discourse about God. A theotelepathy, then, is the experience of the love of God engendered by Him for another person at a distance. We can reach the needs of others by communication with God, who is more passionately concerned than we are.

"For who among men knows the thoughts of a man except the spirit of the man which is in him? Even so the thoughts of God no one knows except the Spirit of God. Now we have received, not the spirit of the world, but the Spirit who is from God, that we might know the things freely given to us by God, which things we also speak, not in words taught by human wisdom, but in those taught by the Spirit...."
I Corinthians 2:11-13, ASV

The Character Transplant

"For me, 'twas not the truth you taught
To you so clear, to me so dim;
But when you came to me, you brought
A sense of Him.

And from your eyes He beckons me
And from your heart His love is shed
Till I lose sight of you and see
The Christ instead."

The greatest gift we can give our friends is to know Christ better than we know them. When Christ takes up residence in us, He performs a character transplant. He makes us like Himself. The fruit of the Spirit, which Paul describes in Galatians 5:22-23, is really a discription of Christ in us. Our friends need from us love, joy, peace, patience, kindness, goodness, faithfulness, gentleness and self-control.

We cannot produce these qualities so necessary to friendship. They are imputed, infused by the indwelling Christ. What He desires to give our friends through us, He inspires in us.

"The mystery which has been hidden from the past ages and generations; but has now been manifested to His saints....which is Christ in you, the hope of glory."

Colossians 1:26-27, ASV

GIFT BOOKS FOR ALL OCCASIONS BY
LLOYD JOHN OGILVIE

- *BEAUTY OF CARING*
- *BEAUTY OF SHARING*
- *BEAUTY OF FRIENDSHIP*
- *BEAUTY OF LOVE*

OTHER BOOKS BY
LLOYD JOHN OGILVIE:

- *GOD'S BEST FOR MY LIFE (A day-by-day devotional)*
- *DISCOVERING GOD'S WILL IN YOUR LIFE*
- *FREEDOM IN THE SPIRIT*

Available at your local bookstore or:

Harvest House Publishers
1075 Arrowsmith
Eugene, OR 97402

Photo Credits:

Scoti Domeij; pages 15, 19, 23, 47

William Jensen; pages 11, 59

All other photos by
Koechel/Peterson Design